A C[illegible]n Tale

[illegible] the

Rubbe[illegible]an

retold by Malorie Blackman

illustrated by Sarah Warburton

Goodness me, but Anansi was lazy! Lazy! LAZY!

When the rains came and all the other men went out to weed and dig and plant their crops, Anansi groaned. The coming of the rains meant the beginning of work – and he hated that.

Anansi's wife said, "Anansi, when are you going to start work on our farm?"

"Soon! Soon!" Anansi yawned. And he turned over and went back to sleep.

The days came and went until Anansi's wife had had enough. "Tomorrow, we'll both go to work on our farm."

"No need. I was going to start work tomorrow actually," said Anansi, quickly. "But if you really want to help, you can buy some groundnuts for planting."

Anansi's wife smiled. At last Anansi was going to do some work!

"And can you roast them and salt them before I plant them?" Anansi continued.

His wife frowned. "No one roasts and salts nuts unless they're going to eat them afterwards."

"Silly! Of course I'm not going to eat them," replied Anansi. "But if I plant them in the ground roasted and salted then, come harvest time, we won't have to cook them. They'll come out of the ground already roasted and salted. It makes perfect sense!"

Anansi's wife wasn't too sure about that but she reckoned Anansi knew more about farming than she did, so off she went to buy the groundnuts.

The next day, Anansi set off with his sack filled with nuts. But did he go to his farm to weed and rake and dig and plant? Of course not! He travelled into the bush to where he wouldn't be disturbed. Then he sat down and guzzled the groundnuts – every one! Only when his sack was empty and his stomach was full, did Anansi stop.

Every morning for the next two weeks, Anansi left the house with a sack filled with roasted, salted groundnuts. He returned each evening with an empty sack and a full stomach.

But time passed as it always does. The seasons came, the seasons went and at last all the farmers in the village began to harvest their crop. All of them, except one.

"We'll go to our farm this weekend and work together," said Anansi's wife. "I'm looking forward to digging up already roasted and salted groundnuts."

Now Anansi was in trouble. How was he going to take his wife to a farm to gather nuts when he'd done absolutely nothing all summer long?

And that's when Anansi had an idea.

The chief of the village had fields full of all kinds of different crops, including *groundnuts*! So later that night, when his wife was fast asleep, Anansi crept out of the house and headed straight for the chief's farm. Anansi started digging up groundnuts and filling his sack. Then he hid the sack in the bush where no one would find it and he went home.

Anansi slept all the next day under his favourite tree, before going home in the evening with his stolen nuts.

"Yuck! These nuts aren't roasted and salted," said his wife, spitting them out.

"Of course not. We only did that to keep the insects away," said Anansi.

That night, Anansi crept out when the sun was down and his wife was fast

asleep and stole as many of the chief's nuts as he could get in his sack. He hid them and tiptoed back into his house, grinning at how very clever he was.

But the following morning, the chief's servant realised that someone had been stealing the chief's groundnuts. And Anansi's luck finally ran out.

"Oh, so there's a thief in the village, is there?" the servant muttered. "Well, I'll find out who you are, you just see if . I don't."

The servant used calabashes to gather sap from all the rubber trees. Then he shaped the rubber sap like a man. He put the rubber man in the middle of the groundnut field and left it standing there in the hot sun.

That night, Anansi sneaked out of the house and headed straight for the chief's groundnut field. He started gathering up more nuts but then he turned around. Arrggghhhh! Oh no! What a shock! There was already someone in the field.

"Wh-who are you?" Anansi trembled.

The rubber man didn't speak. In the darkness, Anansi couldn't see that the man wasn't real. All he knew was that there was a shadowy figure standing in the middle of the field watching him and not saying a word.

"Speak up!" Anansi blustered. "What are you doing here?"

But of course the rubber man couldn't speak. Anansi grew so angry he tried to push the rubber man over. Big mistake! The rubber man had been out in the sun all day so he was icky and sticky and Anansi's hand stuck to his head.

"Let me go at once!" Anansi demanded. He tried to use his other hand to push against the rubber man's chest, but that stuck fast too. Anansi was desperate now. He kicked at the man to try and free himself, but his feet stuck to the rubber man's legs. Frantic, Anansi tried to use his head to push away from the rubber man but that didn't work either. Anansi was well and truly stuck. Only when he couldn't move a single part of his body did he realise that he'd been tricked.

"Now everyone will know I'm a thief," Anansi thought miserably.

But there was nothing he could do about it.

The next morning, the servant came with all the village elders to see who had been stealing the chief's groundnuts.

"Ho! So it was you, Anansi!" said the servant. "I should have guessed."

Anansi was taken to the chief while drummers proclaimed near and far that Anansi was a thief.

Anansi was so ashamed that when he got home he hid up in the corner of the room. And that is where Anansi the spider man's descendants can be found to this day – hiding in the corner of rooms, away from everyone else's gaze.

That's exactly how it happened.
I know! I was there!